WHY HAPPINESS IS THE WAY TO GO

BESTSELLING AUTHOR
CLARENCE KD MCNAIR

Copyright © 2020 by Clarence McNair

All rights reserved. No part of this publication may be used or reproduced by any means, electronic, mechanical, graphic, including photocopying, recording, taping or by any information storage retrieval system or otherwise be copied for public or private use – other than "fair use" as brief quotations within articles and reviews - without prior written permission of the copyright owner.

ISBN-13: 978-1-7341797-6-7

This book was printed in the United States of America

For information regarding special discounts for bulk purchases, please contact the publisher:

LaBoo Publishing Enterprise, LLC
staff@laboopublishing.com
www.laboopublishing.com

Scripture quotations marked (NIV) are taken from the Holy Bible, New International Version®, NIV®. Copyright © 1973, 1978, 1984, 2011 by Biblica, Inc.™ Used by permission of Zondervan. All rights reserved worldwide. www.zondervan.com

The Holy Bible, King James Version. Cambridge Edition: 1769; *King James Bible Online*, 2019. www.kingjamesbibleonline.org.

Table of Contents

Introduction vii

Foreword ix

Acknowledgments xiii

Chapter 1: Why Them and Not Me? 1

Chapter 2: Face-to-Face with Reality. 5

Chapter 3: Set Yourself Free 13

Chapter 4: What You Say Daily to Yourself Matters 17

Chapter 5: Count Your Blessings 23

Chapter 6: Asking for Help Makes You Cool 31

Chapter 7: Protecting Your Peace of Mind 37

Chapter 8: Running Away from Yourself 43

Chapter 9: A Conversation with a Rich Homeless Man . . . 47

Chapter 10: Killed by Words – The Power of the Tongue. . .51

Chapter 11: No 59

Chapter 12: There Are Two Sides to Every Journey. 63

Chapter 13: Choices and Decisions 67

The 90 Day Plan 73

Afterword 81

Notes 85

Dedication

This book is dedicated to **you**. I hope it transforms you. If you purchased my first book, *Give It One More Try*, I thank you for following me on this journey. I wanted to write this second book because I felt as though it was important after the first book that talked about giving life one more try. Now that you've decided to give life one more try, let's place value on your happiness, because you cannot afford not to. To all my readers who continue to see the value in working on yourself, without you, I would not be where I'm at today, and that's walking in my purpose. It took me many years, many obstacles, and many challenges to get here, but I'm happy I'm here for you. I appreciate my readers; you mean the world to me.

Introduction

Most of us are more aware of how much money we have in the bank, the four seasons, and the weather, than we are of the tension in our own lives, which could be one of the reasons you feel something is missing in your life. For most of us, it's the lack of happiness, whether we realize it or not. The question is: where did it go? Did I give up my happiness? For some people, their happiness has been taken away from them because they didn't realize they allowed the people in their lives to drain the happiness right out of them like a vacuum. We experience frustration from four sources: our environment, our body, our thoughts, and our relationships, which ultimately effects our level of happiness.

I wanted to write this book to open your eyes to why happiness is the way to go, and why it's worth protecting it and fighting for.

I know that some of you reading this may ask why it's important to fight for happiness, and the answer is simple: sometimes, life throws many punches at you, and you never know when you will need to fight to keep your happiness. Sometimes in life, we must put a little bit of work into maintaining the things we have that are dear to us because that's how life goes. Anything that you value, you will take care of, protect, and guard with all your heart. Unfortunately, for most of us, we have not done this as it relates to our happiness.

I hope you are moving closer to understanding that without truly being happy, life is just a big empty race, continuously running and running, trying to fill a void that will never be filled because internally, something is missing. There are some things in your life and some behaviors that need to be fixed. After reading this book, I hope you have a new, profound respect for happiness, and get a better understanding of the things that could be causing unhappiness, along with ways to protect your happiness and understand why the first step is to simply go out and find help. Now, grab a cup of tea or coffee, or some hot chocolate, get comfortable, relax, and walk with me on this journey to understanding why happiness is the way to go.

Foreword

Congratulations, you want to be happy; therefore, you are doing something about it! Many people want something different but get stuck by their fears and never move beyond the wanting. This book is an easy read but not about temporary change, this is about changing your mindset, which is a lifestyle! However, to change in a healthy way, it requires putting yourself first, and putting yourself first means learning how to be happy! Scientist have determined that your happiness level comes from your behaviors and the way you live. If you are broken and don't know where to begin, this book has a message for you. Clarence "KD" McNair is an expert at overcoming the odds and being steadfast in happiness! Elevating people is his gift, married with his many talents as an author, artist, producer, and deemed native son of Baltimore! Usually forewords are tender, relatively simple; however, I want to let you know, KD keeps it real. So, get ready to work, to change, and grow. I'm also warning you to be prepared because everyone in your life isn't ready for change, unless they also read this book. So, be prepared to lose some friends because people will feel abandoned when you no longer want to live life the same way after you've read this book.

The truth is, we are making more money and staying internally broke. This is not a new discovery, but now, more than ever, clinical depression is at an all-time high, and people are ten times more likely to suffer from depression. People are hurt and find comfort in polarizing pain. Our trauma tells us a lie, that "fight or fight" is the only way to stay safe. Yes, we need to know how to protect ourselves from danger, but many of us never turn our "fight or fight" off. So, this book is timely and will save lives. We need to learn how to be happy, and we need to believe we deserve it!

Learning how to be happy takes commitment to the process, which is hard work; it's not only about wishing for more or being lucky. You must have a positive mindset. Studies find that those who think positively, double their chances of finding happiness. Your mind is a muscle that must be trained to be happy. Developing a positive mindset and saying affirmations daily is important. This training starts with increasing your awareness about past trauma, pain, and hurt, then releasing it from your narrative. The past is real but the other key to chasing your happiness is not allowing the past to hijack your present situation, letting your happiness out pace your pain is critical to maintaining your joy.

Foreword

The longest study on happiness by Harvard on Adult Development Researcher, collects information on mental and physical health. Close relationships, more than money or fame, are what keep people happy throughout their lives, the study revealed that relationships and connections are important. I believe good relationships are the foundation to having peace of mind and that they center us. Developing relationships and understanding our gifts allows us to be patient with our mistakes, and love ourselves more and focus on our flaws less.

Use this book to support the exploration of your happiness, emotional intelligence, how to live in the moment, and developing your purpose. Positive psychology teaches us to live moment by moment. Embrace this moment to be happy!

KD is giving a voice to mental and physical health from a unique perspective. Take it, embrace it, and let it change your life. Live Free. Don't worry, get happy!

Lanada Williams, MA, LPC, LCPC is a licensed psychotherapist and mental health consultant and founder of Alliance Family Solutions, a private Telehealth practice.

Acknowledgments

I want to thank God for giving me my gift of understanding, vision, and thought.

To my readers and supporters: thank you. None of this is possible without you.

I especially thank life because it has taught me so many things. Most of us don't understand life; however, with time, things get increasingly clearer when it comes to life. I've witnessed so many people work so hard to make a lot of money, yet true happiness was not a friend of theirs. I wrote this book for everyone because everyone deserves the opportunity to choose what direction they want to go. However, if you picked up this book, I know you are considering making some significant decisions for your life, and I thank you for picking my book up because it's for you. It took many long and sleepless nights, and long hours to complete this second book; however, I had to do it for my readers and anyone looking to

Why Happiness Is The Way To Go

understand why happiness is the way to go. Remember, life is driven by action and today, you took the first steps to a new beginning. There were some amazing people who played a significant role in my journey, one of them being, Lucinda Bassett, who wrote the book titled, *Midwest Center Stress and Anxiety Guide*. I never met her in person; however, at 2 A.M. in the morning, in 2006, it was her commercial that started my transition into understanding what was going on with me at one of the toughest times in my life. Therefore, I thank her so much for her program, which I had ordered after hearing her message on TV. She helped me get through some horrible times. I believe at that moment, God sent her my way. To my hometown friend, Sencera, thank you for always picking up the phone when I needed someone to talk to. To Bishop T. D. Jakes, thank you. Your messages from God where life-changing, and I spent many days watching you on YouTube along this journey.

Thanks to my book family, Kimmoly LaBoo—you're a gift from God.

To Akil Taffe, thank you for always being very organic and real. You are a blessing, my brother. Thank you, Eric Cozier, for always seeing the possibilities in me. Thank you, TV One and Sister Circle Live, for introducing to the world and showing love to my youngest newborn son, Marley. My family and

Acknowledgments

I greatly appreciate that. Finally, I want to thank all the people in the world who decided to give it one more try, after all you've been through.

CHAPTER 1

Why Them and Not Me?

Do you ever wonder why some people seem to have it going on? What makes them so fortunate? The one thing that could be separating you from them is because they choose to be happy. Some of you might think, this is nuts, what is this guy talking about? First, how can I even ever truly be happy with all that I have been through and with everything that has happened to me? At this point in my life, who cares about being happy? It hasn't worked for me ever. Maybe some people are just lucky. And what exactly does it mean to be happy anyway? Many happy people are lonely, and many happy people are lost. OK, that may be your response, but I'm going to open your eyes to a whole new world. Now, grab some tea or coffee, and walk with me as I show you the benefits of being happy and why happiness is the way to go.

Next, **gratefulness**. You must be grateful for the things you have in your life. Sometimes, we walk around so used to the things that are always available to us, and most of the time, we end up taking them for granted. Let's think about the sun. For years and years, the sun has been shining bright. What if one day, we woke up and the sun just stop shining? Don't you think it would scare the heck out of you? Yes, but if it was to start shining again, it would force you to have a higher level of gratefulness for its presence and the contribution that the sun makes to the earth. Let's look at the people around us, having our basic needs met, food, water, clothing, shelter. Sometimes, we take these things for granted until one day, they're gone, and you no longer have them anymore. Many people found gratefulness amid their struggles, realizing that at one point, they had it all and took it for granted. Before I continue, let's look up the word grateful. To be grateful means to show appreciation. Example, I'm very grateful to you for all your help. So, let's be honest with ourselves; have you been grateful? Have you taken the time to look around and realize there's always a reason to be grateful for something even if it seems that life is falling apart? There is always something to be grateful for, even in hard dark times. The problem is, we tend to get lost in our emotions versus paying attention to our situation a little bit closer, forgetting that there is always someone who wishes they could walk in our shoes. Once we realize that gratefulness is one of the key components to happiness, we will understand why happiness attacks company, opportunity, success, friendships, growth, and love. At the end of the day, let's just face the facts; happiness is the way to go.

Now, let's talk about **people**. They say "happy wife, happy life". Sorry to let so many of you down, sorry to hurt your feelings, sorry to disappoint you, but that's wrong. I know some of you may argue; however, let's take a deeper look at that. They say if the other person is happy, then they have a happy life. I beg to differ. The saying should be, "happy you, happy life" because if you're not happy, how can you make someone else happy? Happiness is a state of mind, and when you're happy, everything about you comes across as happy. Therefore, in your relationships, love life, the people around you, and the person that your intimate with will have no other choice but to reap the benefits of you being happy. Society promotes happiness based upon other people, the things you have, your level of success, how many social media followers you have, and how many likes you get from people. The truth is, none of that determines happiness because all these things can come and go and blow away just like the wind. The lesson to be learned is this: never look for happiness in people and things. True happiness comes from within. In a relationship, when you have two people who are independently happy outside of their relationship, that relationship is like fireworks, not because it's one-sided but because both parties are happy. Stick with me, I'm not done yet, we are just getting started. My goal is to change your perspective and open your eyes to why being happy is the way to go, and why happiness attracts company.

Health. Let's talk about the power of being happy when it comes to health. Scientific evidence suggests that being happy may have significant benefits for your health. For starters, being happy promotes a healthy lifestyle. It may also help combat stress, boost your immune system, protect your heart, and reduce pain. What's more, it may even increase your life expectancy. Are you still not convinced that happy is the way to go? Happiness has also been linked to better decision-making and improved creativity. So, rather than success being the key to happiness, research shows that happiness could be the key to success, but perhaps most importantly, people who are happier are more likely to make a positive contribution to society.

 Trying to live a happy life is not about pretending to feel joy all the time. We all come across many problems and it's completely natural for us to feel anger, sadness, frustration, and other negative emotions. It's just part of being a human.

Happiness is about being able to make the most of the good times, but also, to cope effectively with the bad times so that we can experience the best possible life.

Aristotle said, Happiness is the meaning in the purpose of life, the whole being of human existence.

CHAPTER 2

Face-to-Face with Reality

Now that I've got your attention, let's have a real conversation. I hope you've still got your cup of tea or coffee. I'm not done with you yet. In my last book, *Give It One More Try*, I mention that the best moment of my life was when I hit rock bottom. It was the time when I didn't have any friends, so I had to befriend myself. This time of isolation birthed my self-discovery. A lot of the time we are on the go and never stop to take a moment and discover who we truly are because once we discover who we truly are, then we start the process of living out our full truth. One of the biggest challenges in society is being able to be someone you're not and still being happy, because true happiness comes when we release and let go of all the data that we have put inside our brain from external influences and what others have named us. Until you come face-to-face with yourself and start to truly work on yourself, being happy will always be a mystery to you because it will feel impossible.

At this point, I'm certain that you're wondering what is so different about happiness anyway, and the answer is: plenty.

1. Happy people are more likely to achieve success.

2. Happy people get sick less.

3. Happy people tend to attract more friends and associates.

4. Happy people give more to others, and giving more to others has been proven to contribute to more happiness.

5. Happy people are more approachable.

6. Happy people have a more positive attitude, which helps make life simpler.

7. Happy people have a positive influence on their loved ones.

8. Happy people enjoy deeper talks.

9. Happy people smile more.

10. Happy people exercise more and eat healthier because they tend to have a great appreciation for their body.

11. Happy people are happier with what they have and are less likely to become jealous of others.

The happiest people around us know that hating on others is a waste of time, and if things don't go their way all the time, that's OK. When you're happy, you're less likely to stress about wanting more, being jealous of others, or about trying to keep up with the Joneses. Being happy with what you've got will allow you to focus on living your life to the fullest—a life that is meaningful to you.

For years, I wondered what people around me thought about me. For years, every single day, my happiness revolved around other people. For years, I had given up my happiness. For years, I had become numb. For years, I tried to do things to make others happy, hoping that if I could make them happy, it would keep me from being unhappy. The truth is, you cannot change people; a person must want to change for themselves, and trying to change people makes life very miserable within itself. We pray, we talk to people, we try to communicate, we tell them they need to get help, and so we drain ourselves trying to direct people to freedom not realizing that happiness is a state of mind. What I realized was that until that person worked on their mind, there was no way I could do anything to make them happy. Some people have so much luggage buried in a trunk, or should I say junk in a closet, that if they were to open the closet door, they would be buried alive in their own mess. Growing up in a family that had minimum resources, we relied on our faith, and I know some of you may be faith-driven, while some of you may not, but the reality is that we must reach above our higher self. I used to wonder why so many people who have millions of dollars and were extremely successful had committed suicide. For years, that has been the big question for me. l remember thinking about that when I was younger, and it took some time because I wanted to do some research on that. I didn't want to be someone who just read the news and said, "Oh, another millionaire or another celebrity committed suicide." I wanted to take a deeper look and do some research on why. What I discovered was that money and fame did not make them any happier. The truth is, whether you're on top or the bottom, the state of your mind and your level of gratefulness will determine how you perceive and look at life, which ultimately impacts your ability to be happy.

Face-to-Face with Reality

OK, so hopefully, you're starting to warm up a little bit about this big thing called happy. Now that I think that I have your attention, let's talk about signs of an unhappy person. In my opinion, and from what I have experienced in my life, the first sign of an unhappy person is someone who constantly complains. Have you ever met a person who does nothing but complain? They can have their health, cars, they can have the house they want, healthy kids, food in the refrigerator, a job, and yet, they still find reasons to complain. When encountering these people, I recommend that you limit your access to this kind of behavior. For those of you who have loved ones and family members who are never happy, I recommend that you have set days that they can have a minute or two of your time, no more than that. If it gets out of control, I recommend that you put them on pause for a moment. Hope this didn't go over your head but it's true; when you're in the presence of unhappy people, no matter what you do, no matter what you say, it doesn't guarantee that they will be happy because when a person is unhappy, they see life through an unhappy lens. I also want to say this: I did not write this book to put those who may suffer from medical issues down. l understand that some people have chemical imbalances and health reasons that make it extremely challenging for them to be happy, and for them, there is help. We have psychologist and medical doctors who work to try and bring relief to those who suffer from mental illness. l needed those resources very badly along my journey to happiness in overcoming anxiety, depression, and panic, so I understand. Happiness for some is more than just getting advice from reading a book; however, I wrote this book just to address the issues in society due to many people simply not being happy. At the end of the day, everyone wants love. Even during the holidays, people become depressed. What I realized is that a lot of times, our happiness is tied up in people who are no longer with us anymore, or the high-paying job we have, or when we want to buy the family everything that they want. However, what we don't realize is that we have numbed and covered up the truth because for years, we managed to buy happiness through others and things. This doesn't last long, whether you give, whether you find love, or whether you fall in love with the "perfect person", you will realize that the only way you can truly stay happy is to first be happy within yourself.

If you're still with me, let's continue to read together. If you need a minute to get another cup of coffee or tea, or maybe even pop some popcorn, put the book down and then come back. If not, let's continue. It takes more than positive thinking to be happy. Some of the best psychologists and great minds recognize that it takes action, meaning that you must be ready and willing to put some work in to get the results you want. It is the same as not seeing your muscles increase or not seeing your weight drop without doing the work. You cannot see the improvement in your mental and emotional state if you do not put in the work. You must put the work in to see the results. Often, people tell you to cheer up, and they say that time will heal all wounds. However, that's not always the case. Time only works when you use it wisely. In life, sometimes finding love and happiness is like looking for a 9-to-5 job. However, once you become happy, you have a better chance of attracting it, and you don't have to go out looking for it.

So many relationships have gone downhill but not because there was miscommunication, or a lack of understanding, or that they were simply not meant to be. One of the biggest problems has always been unhappiness, and for so many people, happiness means different things. However, true happiness is within; it's not attached to anything. It comes from a level of contentment and gratefulness and having a clear understanding that life is a gift. You only get one life, so it's important to understand that no matter what, time is going to move forward, whether you are happy or sad. Once you understand these things, it should put fire under you to get up and choose to be happy.

CHAPTER 3

Set Yourself Free

When I think about how many people have decided—for selfish reasons—not to be happy, it hurts me to know that a person can be so selfish that they're not even willing to give their own life a chance. Many people have had many losses, and many have walked away from the things that once made them happy. They felt that these moments set the stage for their entire life, and five, ten, fifteen years later, they were still unhappy. They allowed their past experiences to hold them hostage in the prison of unhappiness because they decided to give up their right to be happy. From this decision, everything around you suffers, including your family, your children, your marriage, your relationships, your career, and if you never get help, unfortunately, unhappiness can start to affect your health. Are you still not convinced why happiness is the way to go? So, let me ask you a question: If you could just choose one, would you choose happiness or a long life?

Let's look at more facts. According to the *Positive Psychology Center* website, striving for well-being will allow you to perform better at work, have better relationships, a stronger immune system, fewer sleep problems, lower levels of burnout, better physical health, and you'll live longer. Are you still not convinced why happiness is the way to go? OK, just a little bit more. Being happy promotes a range of lifestyle habits that are important for overall health. Happy people tend to eat healthier, including higher intakes of fruits, vegetables, and whole grains. I know some of you believe that when you're happy, you eat donuts and cupcakes and a lot of other things you shouldn't eat, but research says different.

For those of you who are saying, "Well, the book sounds great but I'm still not happy. You talk a lot about happiness and for some reason, I'm still not able to find happiness or feel happy." For those of you who feel this way, I must remind you that I am not a medical doctor nor can I give you medical advice. However, I will provide you with researchable information in here. There is also something I want you to consider, according to *Medical News Today*, "sadness is a normal human emotion that every person will experience at stressful or somber times. Several life events can leave people feeling sad or unhappy. The loss or absence of a loved one, divorce, loss of a job or income, financial trouble, or issues at home can all affect your mood in a negative way. Failing an exam, not getting a job, or experiencing other disappointing events can also trigger sadness. However, when a person experiences sadness, they can usually find some relief from crying, venting, or talking out frustrations. Often, sadness has links to specific triggers. Sadness usually passes with time, but if it does not or if the person becomes unable to resume normal functioning, this can be a sign of depression. If low moods get worse or last longer than two weeks, the person should talk to a doctor." Always keep this in mind as it relates to happiness and unhappiness. Sometimes, we need to take the extra step to get to happy, and it may require more than just reading a book. I just wanted to remind you of this, so please consider it.

You only get one life to live, so live it to the fullest. Many people have heard this millions of times, but have we really stopped and paid attention and looked at what that means? Some people go through their entire life just existing and not living. For a long time, I realized that I was using a lot of energy when trying to get others to see what I saw in life. At an early age, I realized that the only thing that mattered in life was happiness, because happiness is the foundation to life as life is the foundation to love. Just think about it. If you get one life and you know in the back of your mind and in your heart that this is it, this is all you'll get, doesn't it make sense to live the best life possible, to embrace your happiness, to embrace love, to embrace affection and everything life has to offer? Have you ever just taken a moment and sat with yourself? Why is it that so many people allow themselves to stay unhappy when there is no benefit to unhappiness? The only thing you get out of unhappiness is destruction. They say misery loves company. Well, at some point, misery will run out of space and will start recruiting more territory, meaning attacking more happy people in the hopes that they can influence or talk you out of your happiness. The requirements are that you must come to the table full of complaints and full of problems that you choose not to fix. You must come to the table very ungrateful, and not see the blessings in day-to-day life. To be invited in with the unhappy and keep their company, you must speak the language that they speak. This is my point.

CHAPTER 4

What You Say Daily to Yourself Matters

I need you to tell yourself these things every day, and repeat them every day. If it's challenging to repeat these, at least start with three a day.

1. I will not let other people control my happiness.

2. I will not look to others to make me happy.

3. Before I can be a blessing to someone, I must work on myself first.

4. Everyone deserves a fresh start in life. I am not a victim of my past mistakes and failures.

5. No matter where I go, I meet myself there. Therefore, I have no choice but to love myself first.

6. Working on myself will increase my value.

7. Before a breakthrough can occur, there's always a season of preparation.

8. Time only works when you use it wisely.

9. I may not be where I want to be right now but every single day, I'm getting closer and closer to my goals.

10. I will be under construction my entire life as there's always improvement needed in this game called life.

11. It's OK to ask for help.

12. Life is what I make of it.

13. I will not go another day without fighting for my happiness.

14. The most valuable thing on this earth is my peace of mind; everything else comes second.

15. Happiness is letting go of what I think my life is supposed to look like.

16. The only thing that will make me happy is being happy with who I am and not who people think I am.

17. Happiness comes from my own actions.

18. The key to being happy is knowing that I can choose what to accept and what to get rid of.

19. Learning to say no will save me a lot of headaches.

20. I will quit sacrificing my happiness for others.

21. Change will not kill me; I will stop being afraid of it.

22. I will remember to pray.

23. When I'm happy, I'll produce happiness.

24. I deserve a day to do absolutely nothing.

25. I will not be fooled by people's BS. If they want to make things better, they have the choice to communicate.

26. It's OK to see a psychologist. I won't be embarrassed about it.

27. I did not ask to come into this world, so if I was born into a dysfunctional family, it's not my fault.

28. Being busy and looking busy on social media does nothing for my pockets. I must be productive to see fruit.

29. Before I do anything, I will always weigh the pros and the cons and then make my decision.

30. No one is perfect, so I will stop lying to myself. We all need help.

OK, so after repeating these 30 daily reminders, I'm going to give you some rules that I believe will be an asset to your life.

Rules that will benefit you:

1. Never compare yourself to others, everyone has their own thumbprint.

2. Smile, life is a gift enjoy it.

What You Say Daily to Yourself Matters

3. Never lose your inner child.

4. Don't chase material things, just let them be the fruit of your hard work.

5. Live with gratitude.

6. Make time to get in touch with yourself.

7. Don't look down on failure, it's the best education.

8. Be your biggest fan.

9. Enjoy your success, you worked for it, so turn up.

10. Live in the moment, tomorrow has not happened yet.

11. Surround yourself with people that make you feel good. If you're in a toxic relationship, then you have the choice to get out of it. You deserve the right to be happy.

12. Read this book until it sticks with you.

13. If you can't afford it, then you don't need it. Try your best to stay out of debt. It plays a major part in your happiness.

14. Never try to control others, people are who they are.

15. Don't expect people to believe in you. As long as you believe, that's all that matters.

16. Enjoy your time in the shower, there is power in water.

17. Do not live your life to please others, it will quickly send you into unhappiness.

18. Don't take life too seriously, live. It's OK to smile.

19. Don't expect people to be happy for you when you accomplish something big because unhappy people don't produce happiness, they produce hate.

20. Remember you're only one person. You can't take on the world by yourself, so stop trying.

21. Fall in love with the word no.

CHAPTER 5

Count Your Blessings

The power of counting your blessings. I remember thinking back on the moments when I hit rock bottom and when I didn't even have money to put gas in the car. It was rough. However, growing up, I used to hear the older people say, "Well, at least we have food, at least we have water." I would think about my grandmother who never complained. She just talked about how grateful she was to God that she could see another day. My bottom line is that one of the biggest reasons we sometimes feel unhappy or even sad is because we're not counting our blessings. We wake up every day focused on the things we lack and believe that our happiness is solely dependent on achieving the next big thing. Because of my grandmother, I could see life differently from what my circumstances were. Some people would look at me and say, "How do you even smile? You don't have anything." I remember those days, and looking back, I would respond saying, "I have a lot." I'm sure there is someone sleeping on the streets that would love to sleep on a couch and have some heat instead. My point is that counting your blessings, whether they are big or small, can carry you a long way and ultimately, contribute to extreme happiness because it forces you to look at life from a realistic lens, one based on gratitude and understanding that there's always someone who would love to walk in your shoes, and not a lens based on selfishness.

On your journey to happiness, be very careful when encountering people who don't know that they're unhappy. These are the type of people who will destroy everyone's lives around them without even realizing it. These are the type of people who have built a life from misery and brokenness. The worst thing is when a person does not see or believe that they need help. So many people have been drained trying to please these people; trying to compromise for them, and bending over backwards only to receive the biggest smack in the face by the ungratefulness coming from them. These are the people who constantly refuse to work on themselves and have not come to grips that they need help. The great part about life is that we have free will; we have the right to choose who we want to be around. So, make your decisions and choose your company wisely.

I know some of you are wondering, "But what should we do about family members?" You cannot always choose your family members, but how do we deal with that? If they're in denial, if they need help, if they're self-destructive, how can you avoid them? It's quite simple. Unfortunately, they say blood is thicker than water; however, they never said you had to bleed to death. Put limitations on your loved ones. Sometimes, you just need to stay away and limit their access to you to protect your peace of mind and ultimately, protect your happiness, because happiness is something you don't want to live without; it will determine if your life will be full of joy or a living hell. So, protect it at all costs.

As I think about it, we come across so many different challenges, obstacles, and experiences in life. We get stabbed, and we are left with little holes in the walls of our hearts that if not fixed, they will eventually lead us downhill. I always tell people that it's not the big things that you have to worry about, it's the little day-to-day things that add up and ultimately, take over you and your ability to move forward. I hope that after reading this, you will start to look at life somewhat differently and will focus on what's important—that is, being a better you and staying happy. Yes, we're human beings, so I understand that you're going to have ups and downs. I understand these things, but at the same time, there's always a reason to smile, there's always something that you can be happy about, and moving forward, I would love for you to focus on happiness and what it means to you. Hopefully, after reading this book, you will have a new, profound meaning and understanding of the power of happiness and why it is the way to go. Millions and millions of Americans and people throughout the world want to be happy, but the problem is, it seems as though finding happiness and staying happy is a mystery. I hope that I can help you get an understanding of the importance of happiness. I'm not saying that my book is a Bible. I'm not saying my book is the blueprint to happiness. All I'm trying to do is turn the lights on in your life so that you can see that some of the things that have been holding you back, some of the problems that you've been having, and some of the career difficulties and disappointments have simply come from your level of happiness. I hope that this will force you to dig deeper into improving yourself, whether it's emotionally, spiritually, or physically. Work on yourself because you only get one body, and life is all about the journey. It's a long journey, and you will be a work in progress for a long time, but it is worth the fight.

Now, let's talk about a big problem that's taking place in society today. Many people simply want to look happy versus being happy. Because of social media, we can create an illusion of happiness, trying to make others think we have a perfect life when in reality no one has a perfect life. The problem with this new way of expression is that it sends many false messages to those who are looking from the other side to the point where some people have become depressed just from being on social media. They wonder what they might be doing wrong by comparing themselves to others and their seemingly perfect lives. However, what we don't realize is that it's all perception. There's a big difference between perception and reality and the reality is, most people's lives are nowhere near perfect, and most people are not perfectly happy. However, social media allows us to create whatever we want people to believe about the life that we have. I sometimes ask myself if maybe we've gotten so far away from truth that people have tricked themselves into accepting the feeling they get when people like their photos on Instagram. Maybe social media is exposing the desperation of people, yelling look at me, look at my perfect life, and I'm super happy but knowing in the back of their mind it's not real. I believe that when you are not being truthful, you get a false sense of happiness. However, this is not to take away from those who are extremely happy, because I do believe there are many people on social media who post exactly what their life is about, and that is real happiness. I am just trying to give some of you a wakeup call. We need to realize that we're not going to be young forever. How long can we keep up the smoke and mirrors, creating false perceptions, realities, lives, and stories simply to mislead people into believing that we're happy?

I believe that if we started to count our blessings, we would have no need to create an illusion, we would simply be who we are and no matter what people thought, it would not be relevant because at the end of the day, we would still be happy.

Now, let's jump into living with gratitude. We live in a society where people want more, more, and more. Sometimes, we forget to even focus on the blessings that we currently have because we get so consumed in looking for the next big house, car, better pair of shoes, cell phone, TV, or piece of jewelry. The list goes on. There's nothing wrong with any of these things or even upgrading. I believe that if you work hard, you should be able to treat yourself and upgrade your life. However, the problem comes when there isn't any gratitude and gratefulness for the things that you already have, because until you conquer gratefulness and learn to be thankful at every level, it's almost impossible to truly be happy. I know many people who have all the things in the world and they're still unhappy. I used to wonder why. People like them felt like the world owed them something. They never thought that one day, things could change and they could end up in a place wishing they had the current situation that you have now.

In my own life, I have experienced seeing miracles and all kinds of blessings happen. Unfortunately, what I realized is that when a person is dealing with their own problems and issues, they can't see the blessings in their life. So, even though they have all their needs met, they still find a reason to complain. I know that we sometimes place expectations on people; however, we must realize that happiness is a state of mind and until that person works on their state of mind and fixing the lens that they see life through, it doesn't matter what happens in their life, they will still be ungrateful and unhappy, they will still complain and will look for the next problem. And what happens as a result? The people around them suffer and become drained. These people are called energy vampires. Energy vampires are people who get life from draining energy from you. Have you been in a great mood and just full of life and then encountered an energy vampire? These are the people that once you come into their presence, they drain the life out of you. This comes from their unhappiness. You leave their presence and suddenly, you're exhausted because they have drained every bit of energy from you. Are you still not convinced why happiness is the way to go?

I once had a neighbor named Mike, and every day, he would come and knock on the door and ask for some work. He would be smiling. All he was looking for was a way to make a couple of dollars to get through the day. He would clean the porch, clean the backyard, or do small paint jobs for $20. So, one day, I asked Mike, "How do you survive by knocking on people's doors? That's not enough money to live on." He replied saying that he didn't do it for the money. Instead, he did it because he loved people and wanted to help the community. The point of this story is simple. For Mike, the focus was not on himself. Instead, the focus was on helping the community. We saved money because Mike asked for a donation and in exchange, he would help keep the community up simply because he was grateful and had a high level of gratitude for the community that we lived in. It was not the best community; however, there were people like Mike who valued what we all had.

I hope you realize that sometimes in life, we can't always do everything for money; we must do things for a higher purpose, a higher meaning, and a higher reason. When we do things from a genuine place, we experience the fullness that life has to offer.

CHAPTER 6

Asking for Help Makes You Cool

One of the biggest challenges in life is to simply ask for help. We go years and years without asking for help, and during those years, we become dangerous to everyone around us, causing people misery, and even sending some into depression from having to deal with us. This has been a personal challenge for me during my years of getting happy. It took me a long time to muster up the strength to ask for help without being embarrassed. It got so bad for me that I had no other choice but to ask for help, and thinking back, I'm so happy that I got help. So, I encourage you to stop walking around and internalizing your problems, childhood traumas, adult traumas, heart breaks, let downs, and disappointments. These are some of the contributing factors as to why you may not be completely happy. When you think about it, there's a lot of time, energy, and effort wasted in being unhappy. Are you still not convinced happiness is the way to go?

I hope I still have your attention. Let's talk about selfishness. Is selfishness robbing you of your happiness? Me, me, me, no matter the age, some people are solely focused on pleasing themselves, and after years of this selfishness, it sometimes comes at a cost to others. Do you honestly think that you could be completely happy when, in fact, everything about your life is based on whatever makes you happy, and never putting others before yourself? I'm not saying that you should not put your needs first. I'm simply talking about being selfish. A lot of the time what we don't realize is that being selfish can take away from being truly happy. If we start to pay attention to our surroundings, I'm sure we will see a world that is in desperate need of any bit of contribution, whether its volunteering time at your local school, or helping the elderly. Whether it's buying someone a coat who could be cold for the winter or even taking food to someone that you know could use it. These are all selfless acts. Many people would look at me and say, "You're always going out of your way for people, you're always doing all this stuff for people. What do you get out of doing that?" I always tell them that I find joy in putting others first and taking the attention off myself. It's not to say that I don't love myself and I should not put myself first; however, sometimes, to get to know yourself and understand yourself, you need to help others because that is when you get to a place where you truly start to understand what life is about. Most of the time, in the process of helping others, you will realize that life is not just about you. Instead, life is about being a human being and being able to be of service to others. I have reaped many benefits from simply paying attention to the needs of others in my daily life. By taking the attention off ourselves and placing it on others, we can help those in need.

Control. What controls my happiness? Have you ever asked yourself that question? For many, it could be their jobs, friendships, or relationships. It could be the clothes they wear. It could be the title or the position of a job. It could be their boss at work or maybe the likes and followers they get on social media. However, have you ever asked yourself, "What controls my happiness?" Or did you go your entire life not paying attention? If so, you might not have realized that some things have been controlling your life; therefore, controlling your happiness, and at any moment, if any of these things were to go, your happiness would go out the door right behind them. Have you ever heard anyone tell someone, "You put your job before your family, you're going to lose your family"? I'm sure you've heard this one before. The reality is that to some people, that is what controls their happiness, and they do not realize that that is the one thing that's destroying their personal life and robbing them of true happiness. Since they built their entire lives around fear, such as fear of not being liked by their boss, etc. I'm not saying you should not care about your boss or your job. Instead, what I'm saying is that when these things start to control your life, then it becomes a problem. What I recommend is to stop letting your fears control your life. To be truly happy, you must be happy within yourself, without needing others' approval. Remember, you're the most powerful tool in your life, so use it wisely or it could cost you your happiness.

So, we can't talk about control without talking about letting go. A lot of your lack of happiness has come from holding onto things that are unhealthy for you, such as bad relationships, bad friendships, or careers that do not allow you to grow. For many of us, letting go is not an easy thing to do. It took me years to finally come to the realization that I had to let go of my past of being a Motown recording artist so that I could grow. I had to move on, but more importantly, I had to let some things go. I've witnessed people who are unable to let some things from the past go. Ultimately, they end up becoming hostage to the things that they would not let go of. What I've come to understand is that one of the reasons it is so hard to let go of something is because we've become identified with them, and, therefore, if we let them go, they will leave us empty. By doing so, we are giving fear way too much power. Fear is said to be false evidence appearing real.

It's time to talk. I recommend that you find someone that you trust or seek professional help. There is power in talking about the things that could be causing your unhappiness. One of the main reasons for your lack of happiness is your lack of communication. I remember I would hold everything in, I would internalize everything, and it was horrible. I think it's very important for you to find someone to talk to, someone that you trust, and someone that you can open up to and be vulnerable and real with. If you keep things inside of you, all the bottled-up emotions will eventually come out. The problem is that you have no clue how they will come out and who will be affected by it. It's always better to find someone to talk to rather than to hold things in. I would always talk about how the mind can have so much going on and no one even knows it. For example, there were two guys who worked in the same department. The guy who had been at the job for 10 years came to work faithfully every single day and made the company a ton of money. However, within the time of him being on the job, the company changed general managers, and the new guy came in and wasn't the nicest guy to get along with. Over time, the new guy rubbed the other guy the wrong way. Instead of expressing himself and talking about it to the general manager, he went home and took it out on his wife. The moral to the story is that it wasn't the wife that he was mad at, it was the boss at the job that he was mad at. However, his wife was the closest person around to take everything out on. How many times do we walk around holding things in, only to take them out on others? The bottom line is that it's time to talk. It's time to stop holding things in. It's time to start communicating and expressing yourself to people. If someone offends you, it's time to have a conversation and sometimes, it's not about the consequences. The bottom line is that it's just about what's right.

CHAPTER 7

Protecting Your Peace of Mind

In this chapter, we're going to talk about protecting your happiness. How do you protect your happiness?

Number one—and this was a hard lesson for me to learn—stop picking up the phone when you know that the person who's calling is only calling you to complain. They don't want a solution to their problem, they just want to complain. So, what ends up happening is that you constantly pick up the phone and you constantly sit with them, you go to dinner with them, without realizing that they don't want any help and eventually, this will start to weigh down on you and start to drain you. What ends up happening is that every time you see that number come up on your phone, you start to get anxious and you'll become thrown off because that person is only calling to dump all that negative energy on you. So, you simply don't pick up the phone. You're not obligated to pick up the phone, especially when you know you offered help and they refused to receive it. That's not your responsibility. At that point, they are in God's hands, and all you can do is simply pray for them. Diving into someone's mess is not going to help them at all, and it won't help you.

Number two. Now, this is something that I learned, but it took me years to understand. Stop giving everyone your *me time*. Meaning, when you need to relax and be alone, stop giving others your *me time*. It doesn't mean that you should check your text messages right away. If it's not an emergency, you don't need to pick up your phone. Put your phone down when you are having *me time*. Don't check your email messages, don't check your text messages, stay off social media, and don't check your voicemail when you are having *me time*. Instead, have *me time*. What you fail to realize is that external energies enter the moment you pick up a device and you get on social media. This will affect your level of relaxation, your levels of peace, and ultimately, depending on what it is that you encounter, will destroy your *me time* and your ability to have peace of mind. For a second, just think about it. Let's say you are sitting at a lake or maybe just listening to your favorite music or taking a walk in the park—anything that you consider relaxing—and then you pick up your phone or you find out that someone had just been shot. Now, you could be in a very pleasant environment or just simply relaxing and having a cup of tea, but the moment you take that information in, it changes your brain chemicals instantly. You can go from being happy to depressed just because of the negative information you see. My point is that when you have *me time*, have *me time and* not me and my phone, not me and my emails, not me and Twitter, not me and Facebook, not me and Instagram time. Simply, have *me time* and take a break. We must realize that the moment we give our attention to anything else, we place ourselves in a very vulnerable position to be distracted or hurt.

Number three. If you want to protect your happiness, you need to be careful of the company you keep. But more importantly, be very careful of the environments you choose to spend your time in.

Number four. Repeat after me: I am not a dumpster; it is not my responsibility to allow people to dump all their trash on me. Once again, I am not a dumpster; it is not my responsibility to constantly take in all your trash. Unfortunately, some people have made a habit of always bringing their trash to you, as though you are their dumpster. Once again, you're not a dumpster to anyone, your job is not to constantly allow people to dump all their waste, their trash, and their drama on you. If you take heed to this, I guarantee that it will contribute to the protection of your happiness because once you gain happiness, you won't want to let people come in and take it away from you. There's nothing wrong with lending an ear to a loved one or friend, but when they reject solutions and advice that could help them and they just want to keep dumping their trash on you, then that person is out of your hands. There's nothing else you can do. You can no longer listen to or absorb any of that negativity, bad energy, and junk.

Now, let's talk about **gratitude**. I'm just going to cut right to it. Whatever it is that you take for granted, will leave your life. If it's a great friendship and you take it for granted, eventually, that friendship will end. If it's a great spouse and you don't show any gratitude or thankfulness toward that person, eventually, they will leave your life. If you had a career opportunity and you weren't appreciative or grateful for the opportunity, eventually, you will lose it. Anything that has been placed in your life that you take for granted, you will lose. And that could be your children, your friends, your aunts, your uncles. That could be anyone who has been supportive, or done everything that they could do to help you. If you take them for granted, eventually, they will be removed from your life. How many times have we said things to people, talked down to people, disrespected people, and took them for granted until one day, we woke up and they were gone, no longer willing to be unappreciated. Many people are walking around unhappy, not because they never found happiness, but because they were ungrateful to the people that were in their lives. Now, they're lonely, they're walking around miserable, and no one wants to be around them. These are the kind of people who, once again, refuse to get help. If only they would just get help and work on themselves, things could be so much better. However, they'd rather walk around and mistreat the people who love them and take them for granted. And we wonder why some people have a hard time finding happiness. How can you find happiness if you're unhappy on the inside? The way you treat people reflects what's going on inside of you. Think about this. I hope that this changes someone's life. I hope that this brings awareness to someone, and I hope that this forces someone to just take a minute and look at themselves in the mirror and decide to become a better you. It's never too late to get it together. However, I'm not saying you will get those relationships back, but at least if you work on yourself and learn to be more appreciative, you will move forward with more gratitude.

So far, I hope that the information in this book is helping you understand why happiness is the way to go. I also hope that this book opens your eyes to how important it is to protect your happiness and how to gain happiness and stay happy. I also hope it helps you understand why some people are not happy. I took some time to dive into understanding happiness, it all boils down to the fact that if you're not happy, then nothing else matters. You can have all the money you want; you can have all of the attention you want; you can have all the likes and followers you want, but until you are internally happy with yourself, none of these things matter. More than likely, you will not even appreciate these things, and nine times out of ten, you'll probably end up losing them or destroying relationships anyway. That is, until you are internally whole.

CHAPTER 8

Running Away from Yourself

Stop running away from yourself. For years and years, I was running away from myself. It took me twenty years to realize that I had been running away from the person that God had designed me to be. He gave me so many gifts that I've buried for so many years, chasing something that I thought would make me whole and make me happy. When I think about it, I was dimming my light. God said, "Let your light shine before men." Well, how are you letting your light shine if you keep running away from it? Many of us have natural gifts and natural abilities that people have noticed in us for years. Whatever that one thing you have is, it is your gift. Perhaps someone has said, "I needed that talk, this is so amazing, or every time you do this it just really brings me joy." See, God has been speaking to us the whole time. The problem is, we tend to try to figure it out for ourselves, and we tend to come up with our own plans and run around trying to make it happen on our own. It took me so many dark moments, so many ups and downs, and so many failed attempts that it almost felt as though God was saying, "OK, you did 1000 things and nothing worked. You might have made a few bucks along the way, but this is not what I designed you for, this is not why I have been protecting you." In that moment, I didn't realize that God was waiting on me to stop running from myself, look at myself, pay attention to myself, and stop trying to be something that I wasn't. Stop trying to live through other people, stop trying to please other people, and stop trying to build an illusion of success because if your success does not come from your gift, it will be short-lived anyway because whatever your gift is, it was given to you by God. So many times, we put it off, we put it off, and we put it off. Sometimes, God will let you run around for years until you get to a place where you have no choice but to look at yourself and stop running around chasing affiliations, stop trying to be in the in-crowd, and stop trying to do what everybody else is doing. Instead, you need to get to a place of self- discovery. For so many years, I would visit family, loved ones, and friends, and I would have conversations with people and they would ask, "How do you understand things the way you do?" Or "I really needed to talk to you. I'm so happy that I could talk to you." Since I was about 15 years old, people would say to me, "You have the mind of an old person." I found it so funny, but never thought anything of it. I always was interested in people, and God gave me the ability to see life with a clear vision. However, the problem was that as I got older, I got further and further away from that because at the same time, I had a musical talent, but as I think back, I feel as though my musical experience happened so that I could have more experiences, meet new people, and encounter different personalities so that I could be more relatable to more people. I must be honest, it's been a long journey., Again, we must stop running from ourselves. So many people are trying to figure out how to become successful, how to become rich, and how to live a life of abundance. So, we have tried 1 million things only to constantly be let down, and even if those things work, we still feel that something is still missing from our lives. Most of the time, you feel empty because you're not operating in your gift, you're not operating in purpose, because in life, to truly be happy, you must become one with yourself. At some point, you need to look at the man in the mirror and find a way to change your way. God lets you exercise your right of free will. He allows you to have a couple of ups and downs and bumps until you wake up and realize that it wasn't as hard as you made it out to be. Life comes with challenges. Life comes with many ups and downs, but truth be told, a lot of these complications are simply because we will not be still for a moment and let God speak to us. People say, "What am I here for? What is my purpose? Why did this happen to me? Why was I born like this? Why, why, why? There are so many why's. However, once you get to a place of purpose, all the questions and all the unknowns will start to reveal themselves. It happened for me when I decided to pick up my pen again and write. By pouring out what was inside of me, it gave me an overflow of happiness, contentment, joy, and satisfaction because now I was blessing others with my gift, and I knew that I could impact someone and possibly even change their life.

CHAPTER 9

A Conversation with a Rich Homeless Man

He had been poor in terms of material things, he didn't have a place to live, he wore the same clothes every day, he lived from house to house and on the streets from time to time, and had minimum food. He wasn't the most popular guy you would want to be around. He didn't have many friends or family or any support at all from a loved one. However, he was rich in ways that most people spend their entire lives trying to get to because this homeless man, through his losses, gained a deeper appreciation and gratitude for the more important things in life. His name was Joe, and in Joe's past life, he worked in corporate America. He made over $750,000 a year, had great benefits, an expense account with a retirement plan that was out of this world, and a 401K big enough to fit into a boat. Joe would be invited to exclusive parties, exclusive dinners, and had tons of friends. He received lots of awards, he drove a S500 Mercedes Benz, and lived in a million-dollar condo, and had enough clothes to dress a high school class. However, without any warning signs, the company went out of business and his high-paying job, the fancy cars, the party invites, and all his friends went out the window, ultimately leaving Joe with nothing because he partied all the time and never thought in a million years that it would all be gone in the blink of an eye.

Joe went from living in a fancy condo to losing everything, and it caused him to become homeless. I know some of you are probably saying, "Well, if he was educated enough to get this corporate job, why didn't he apply for other jobs? Well, this wasn't just a job. Instead, Joe's whole identity was wrapped up into this job, his whole world revolved around this job, and nothing else was more important to him but the praise he received from having it. He was so emotionally invested in this job that when the company went out of business, he could not see himself doing anything else. It was like he had lost everything inside of him. He mentally broke down, he was emotionally torn apart, and ultimately, he lost his self and ended up in a bad place. As the days went by, he fell deeper and deeper into a dark hole. As time went by, he began to reminisce about the days he had everything and wondered whether this was just a bad dream. He began to ask himself, "How did I go from being on top of the world to sleeping in a homeless shelter? What did I do wrong? How could this happen to me? See, during these years of struggle, Joe came face-to-face with himself, and thought about all the times he took his job, car, and house for granted, as well as having clothes, food, and water. More importantly, he took life for granted. It was not until he hit rock bottom that he began to realize that just getting through the day was an accomplishment. Having something to put on your back was a blessing; having a place to lay your head when it was cold outside was even more of a blessing; and having a bus pass to get around was a privilege. Joe started to see life from a totally different perspective. He started to realize that life is a gift, and the things that we take for granted every day because of our desire to have more has blinded us from being able to see the true joys of life like, life itself. See, Joe realized that there was nothing wrong with having all the money and material things in the world; however, when you forget that there are people who are living day to day, meal to meal, and are barely getting by yet are still grateful for all of the little blessings they receive in life, like having a blanket, a place to lay their head, clean water, or any kind of support, was a blessing. When Joe hit rock bottom, he realized how fortunate he was after it was all gone. This experience opened his eyes and it taught him that you can be homeless and still be rich. Maybe not rich in the eyes of America, maybe not rich in ways that most people strive to be; however, they are rich in gratitude, because when you hit rock bottom and you have nothing, you realize every little thing is a blessing. You realize waking up in the morning is a blessing, you realize having food to eat is a blessing, and having a roof over your head is a blessing. Once you understand this and you truly learn the power of gratefulness, life will become so fulfilling and happy that it will feel like a dream because then you'll be aware of what your true needs in life are and everything else is extra. This level of gratefulness births happiness.

CHAPTER 10

Killed by Words – The Power of the Tongue

Let's talk about how words kill people. Think about having a gun; you load it up, and one bullet is rage, one bullet is anger, one bullet is hurt, and one bullet is hate, now think about someone pulling the trigger with all these negative words coming off their tongue. Each negative emotion produces one of these words. Hurt produces certain words, rage produces certain words, and anger produces certain words. When a person shoots these words at you, they can literally kill you. So many people have committed murder and gotten away with it because they were just using words. You can't go to jail for cursing somebody out, but the victim is being tormented, and sometimes, it could lead to physical death. What if there was a place called word jail? Do you realize how many people in the world have been murdered by somebody's words?

Many people have been told by another, "I hate you; you're never going to be anything." Just those words alone can bring so much destruction into your life. It's almost worse than someone shooting you with a gun and physically harming you because when someone speaks these negative and harsh words over your life, it absorbs into your spirit, your soul, your emotions, and it hits you hard mentally. The point of this is that I want you to understand how powerful words are and how words can kill. We need to protect ourselves from anyone, any place, and anything that can shoot us with words. I feel that the same way we promote stop the violence, and stop the crime, I think it's time we start to promote stop the hurtful words, because words kill, no differently than a gun. Proverbs 18:21 (KJV) says, "Death and life are in the power of the tongue", remember what you say can preserve life or destroy it. So, you must accept the consequences of your words.

Taking baby steps in your life all over again

Have you ever heard people say, "Meet people where they are"? Sometimes in life, you need to meet yourself where you are, and when you meet yourself where you are, it helps illuminate that unnecessary stress. Sometimes, when you are having a rough time in life, you just need to tone it down a little bit and come down to reality. Like, I know I want to be here, and I miss how things used to be, but that's not where I'm at right now in my life. I'm here, and in this moment, I am going to learn to embrace the space and work on ways to get out of the situation. Meaning that if I'm at rock bottom, I need to stop comparing myself to others. I need to be OK with the fact that I may just have to continue to take baby steps all over again in my life at this current time. Once we become aware of the truth and get out of our head, we are now able to start rebuilding again. Often, we create these false pictures of ourselves that are not true, and when we fail to live up to this false story in our head, it causes us great unhappiness. I call it being held hostage by your ego.

Your ego is causing too much unhappiness, so it's time to let it go and focus on getting to know your authentic self.

Your ego is basically your own made up identity that you have created in your mind, which is usually not your authentic self. If we take a look at everything we believe about our personality, talents, and abilities, it would not be hard to figure out why so many people become unhappy, because we live our lives trying to create our own identities. Often, these identities are formed from trauma, bad experiences, let down, hurt, disappointment, brokenness, low self-esteem or bad relationships, and then when we create these false identities. We start to believe it to the point where we'd rather suffer in silence than get help because we become afraid of what people might think if they'd ever get to know the real us. I want you to read this part three times and read it very slowly. I think the message is clear that sometimes in life, you have seasons where things are up and things are down, and we have seasons for growth and prosperity. However, how many of you have missed your season simply because you were hiding behind a mask? You must realize there is something special about you that no one else has and sometimes, you just need to start all over and rebuild again. Once you realize that trying to hold onto a false image of yourself is causing you so much unhappiness, then you are able to create change. The key is to honestly recognize there is a problem, and that it's time to get help.

This hit home for me when I was on Jamie Foxx's *Bait* movie soundtrack. I felt like I was 30 feet tall and on top of the world. We had just recorded with a big producer who worked with Janet Jackson (Darrell Delite Allamby from 2000 Watts), and we had gotten paid for the movie soundtrack. I was young and my whole world thrived off my ego. I felt like I had to be perfect because this was my first time achieving something of this magnitude. You couldn't tell me anything. However, once the money ran out, I felt like I had to uphold this image that I had created, and boy, it made me unhappy because on the outside, I was the man, but on the inside, my money had run out and all I had to hold on to was this identity that I had made up. It was so hard for me to meet myself where I was because I was fighting reality. It was not until I came off that high horse that I could start all over again. I hope after reading this that it opens your eyes to the importance of focusing on improving your authentic self so that if you ever need to start over again in life, at least you can truly start from where you are, and that would be your true authentic self.

Sometimes, help can appear to be intimidating

Think about when you're driving your car in the city and some window cleaner guys come up and ask, "Hey, would you like your windows cleaned?" Your windows could be dirty, and deep down inside, you know you need them to be cleaned, and you know that it's much safer to drive with clean windows than to take a chance. However, you are afraid because of the way the two young guys look. They appear to be very intimidating and dangerous. So, you roll your windows up and lock your doors. That's pretty much how we treat everyday life. How many times have people come into our lives to help us see things better, but because of how they look and how they presented themselves, you rejected them? Most people are looking for someone who looks fancy and well put together because this is the image that most people believe the people who could help them the most would have. However, that person may not be willing to help you in the way that you need. Sometimes, we've got to humble ourselves to get the message and the help. My bottom line is that you never know who God will send to you to help. I'm not saying that you should not be cautious; however, often, help will not appear in the form that you expect it to. Hebrews 13:2 (NIV) says, "Do not forget to show hospitality to strangers, for by so doing, some people have shown hospitality to angels without knowing it."

Remember, don't judge a book by its cover because you never know where the help you've been needing is going to come from.

See the blessing in your past

Stop being mad at your past. It represents who you were at that time.

Often, we move on with our lives, and we may be in a different place than where we were years ago, and during that time, we may have been in a relationship, we may have had children from our past relationship; however, I find that so many people are still angry with the person they were in the past as though it was a fresh beef. Years later, people are still mad and angry at themselves and are unable to move on. I want to talk about this because so many people throw their happiness away and waste so much of their lives just being angry about their past when your past is just a reflection of who you were at that time. Meaning that at that time, you may not have been mentally fully developed into the person that you are today. Sometimes, you have to be realistic about your situation even if you are now a very positive person, you may be a very spiritual person, you may work out, eat healthier, or may only want to hang around positive people, and only go out a few times during the year, or maybe you went back to school and got your education, or maybe you lost a loved one and it pushed you to want to change. However, we need to be realistic and understand that we weren't always this way, and during that time of immaturity and when we were making many bad decisions, those people that you attracted were simply just a reflection of that place that used to be. So, whenever you feel the urge to get angry at the people from your past, whether a husband or wife, past friendships, or past coworkers, no matter who, just remember these people, places, and things were all attracted by you, so you can't blame anyone. Sometimes, we make changes in our life and finally get it together, and we expect others to do the same, which is usually not the case. I wanted to write this to save you a lot of heartache, hoping that you would see things differently and realize that sometimes in life, we hit a low point mentally, emotionally, spiritually, and physically, and during those times, we tend to attract people who reflect the image that we have of ourselves. So, be careful with getting upset so fast at the people from your past. More than likely, you see them as the enemy. However, if you could look back in the mirror at that time, you would see yourself as the enemy. When we make life changes, we tend to forget that most people will not be exactly where we are now, but it doesn't mean they won't have their day of change. My point is that sometimes, you've just got to be patient and hope for the best, and understand that the past is simply the past. That doesn't mean that nothing good has come from it because if it were not for those dark moments, whether you knew they were dark or not, you would not be the person you are today.

CHAPTER 11

No

This one word can save your peace of mind; and save you from a lot of problems.

For as many years as I can remember, I spent a lot of time running and running, taking on so many projects, and trying to help so many people. So many people would call and dump all their problems on me. I found myself not being able to get proper rest at night and taking on more than I could chew. One of the hardest things for me was to say "No." It took me years and years to get to a place to finally learn to put myself first, and understand that I could not save everyone or please everyone or even be liked by everyone. It was the moment when I came face-to-face with the reality that there is only one God and that's not me. I realized that I was playing God and trying to be the ultimate fixer of everyone's problems, while neglecting my own challenges and problems, and not realizing that eventually, it would all catch up to me. I can remember the days when I would smile but internally, I was very unhappy because my world revolved around other people's happiness. I took on a job that I was never created to handle and that meant saying yes to everyone, thinking that if I said no, they may not like me anymore or see me differently. I'm sure this part of the book hits home for so many people, including you! You must learn to say no and not allow people to use guilt or manipulation to make you feel that you should not love yourself enough to say no when enough is enough. You can say yes a million times and the time you say no, it's like you never said yes before. That's how people will try to make you feel. Just remember this, your first responsibility is yourself. Even to parents: how can you be a great parent if you're not a great person mentally, physically, emotionally, and spiritually? You must be whole to truly be a blessing to someone else. If you're all out of order, bent out of shape, mentally exhausted, and feeling neglected because all you do is worry about how people will feel about you, view you, or you're so wrapped up in being a people pleaser, how can you have a life if your whole world is so consumed in other people's lives? Do you think that you could stay happy living like this? I don't think so. Therefore, sometimes in life, we need to make some serious decisions and understand why happiness is the way to go.

No

Remember this, people pleasers are very nice people and super helpful, they always make all the fun plans, and are always there for family members and friends. I'm sure a lot of people think that it's the coolest thing when someone is like this; however, it can be extremely unhealthy behavior. Here's a story of a young lady named Linda. She has three kids, four brothers and sisters, a mom and dad, a husband and many so-called friends. When 2018 hit, she made plans to become the best version of herself. However, instead of prioritizing her fitness journey, eating healthy, taking days to rest, and taking more *me time*, Linda ended up finding every excuse in the world not to put herself first because in her mind, if she was not the perfect wife, the perfect sister, the perfect daughter, the perfect friend, the perfect mother, and the perfect person to everyone, she would not be loved. So, Linda never went to the gym. Linda started to gain more weight because of her eating habits. She started to suffer from fatigue and anxiety and from lack of rest from running all over the place taking care of the family, cooking for everyone, and answering the phone every time someone called. Linda ultimately ended up hospitalized from exhaustion, unable to help anyone. Linda was now forced to keep the goals she'd made for herself because at this point, her life depended on it. Linda was a people pleaser, and she was unable to say no. All her time revolved around taking care of other people. So, how could she better herself if her focus was being at everyone's beck and call?

According to psychologists, the intense need to please and care for others is deeply rooted in either a fear of rejection or the underlying feeling that if I don't do everything I can to make this person happy, they might leave or stop caring for me. Fear of rejection can come early in relationships wherein love was conditional, or wherein you were rejected/abandoned by an important person in your life. Maybe a parent left or was emotionally unavailable or inconsistently available. No matter how you put it, fear is the route driving this behavior. I'm not saying you should not be helpful; however, if you don't take care of yourself, how can you be good to anyone else? Think about it. Remember, some people will use you without even thinking twice because they are selfish and have never cared about anyone but themselves. As a people pleaser, you have fallen into their trap. You can't even see it because you're a genuine person and most of the time, these people see your vulnerability and take advantage of it. So, the next time you decide to put yourself last, think about this: you only get one life, so try to love yourself rather than trying to make everyone else happy. I think by now you understand why happiness is the way to go. So, ask yourself: have you been choosing to be happy? If not, I hope this book opens your eyes.

CHAPTER 12

There Are Two Sides to Every Journey

The way we see our journey often is not the way others see it. Now, before you continue to read, I want you to think about what you've read so far because we often spend a lot of time stressed, worried, getting a headache, trying to convince people to see our vision or believe in what we believe in. The reality is you cannot change people. People are going to be people. Sometimes, we get to this place called success, and we become uptight and cold because of how people treated us along the journey. Have you ever heard people say that when they make it, they will cut everybody off; when they make it, they will not help anybody; when they make it, they will move away from everybody; when they get a new job, they don't want anybody asking them for anything? The reality is that people will never see the journey the way you see the journey because it's not them who have the vision. God has given you the vision for your life. The minute you start to convince yourself that they can see what you see, you set yourself up for heartache, disappointment, and pain. Now, think about it, have you ever been in a situation where you might've been sleeping in a one bedroom apartment and your other friends had bigger houses, or they might've had two cars and maybe you had to catch the bus, and they looked down on you? Maybe you had a goal, something you were trying to achieve, but you had to make major sacrifices along the journey, and other people couldn't understand you. They may have talked about you behind your back, they may have put you down, called you a loser, or said you were crazy, or maybe they said you needed to stop, give up, and just get any job you could find. However, what they didn't know is that you had a vision, and not only did you have a vision, you had faith in a vision because you could see it. Something that will save you a lot of unhappiness is when you finally realize that no one will ever see something that was given to you. We must remember that most people don't see the seeds, they see the growth. So, don't look for happiness and don't look for people to cheer you on along your journey. It may not be that they're hating on you or don't support you, or don't want to see you succeed. The bottom line is that some people just have no vision, and they can't see things clearly. For most people, if they can't touch it or see it, it's not possible.

Don't become angry and bitter because others don't see what you see along your journey... Remember that your vision is your vision, and it's the only one that matters. Everyone will have something to say, so let them talk; it's not their business anyway. Remember that how others see your journey has nothing to do with you, and if you lose focus, you will get derailed. That's why you should never make decisions to please others. Remember that it's your life, not everyone else's, regardless of their intentions. Don't allow yourself to make decisions to please others because in the long run, you will regret not going with your gut. After all, you know yourself better than anyone ever will, so the way you see your journey will never be the way other people see your journey or even talk about your journey. They may say you are out of control; you are a bum, your life looks bad where in actuality, the sacrifices you may make along the journey will help get you to where you're headed. However, others won't see it that way, so don't bother explaining to others why you don't have the money to go out on the weekends, or why you don't have the money right now to go shopping, because you're trying to use it for something beneficial. How can we expect anyone to see what we see? This is why when people reach their goals, the people close to them are in shock because based on their perception of what they were doing and what they were seeing, it looked as though life was going downhill. They no longer hung out, became disciplined, stopped partying so much, and became extremely focused. People don't realize that there are two sides to every journey; the one people on the outside see, and the one you see. Remember, never expect people to be happy for you when their perception of your journey does not match up with your beliefs as this will save you from a lot of unhappiness.

CHAPTER 13

Choices and Decisions

We all look back over our life at some point and I'm sure there are some decisions we had made that we aren't happy about. If you didn't know already, life is all about decisions, and they affect so many things in our lives. What we never talk about is the information and experiences that are stored in your mind that could be a significant factor in the decisions you make. A lot of people have fallen into depression and have been hard on themselves all because they look at the decisions they have made in the past and get so frustrated that they feel there's no hope for them. Some have even been suicidal because they felt as though the world was over because they constantly made bad decisions that put them in many bad situations and caused them many problems. However, what so many people fail to realize is that your decisions reflect your experiences. Let me repeat myself, your decisions reflect your experiences. If you grew up in a household where your parents argued all the time and you didn't see love, and instead, you only saw dysfunction and brokenness, then when you get older, you yearn for the love that was missing in your house growing up. Often, you make decisions that fill that void. Example, you could meet a guy or a girl, and they could be bad for you. However, you can't see it because maybe they say the right things to you or maybe they appear to have it all together. But in the back of your mind, you feel that something isn't right but that desire to feel love is stronger than your vision, so you get into a relationship only to find out that the person is a nightmare, and this one decision altered your entire life because you wanted to fill a part of you that you never have before. This happens to us so many times we make decisions, not because it's the right or wrong thing to do but because we make many decisions based on the need to satisfy something internally. Think about this example: you're 28 years old and you rob a bank. Once you get caught, you then ask yourself, "Why did I do it? Why do I keep making bad decisions?" Have you ever considered that the bad decisions started because of your upbringing and growing up in a single-parent home and because your mom didn't have any money? At the age of 13, you were forced to take care of the family by any means necessary, and over the years, you developed a survival mentality and took that into your adulthood. Instead of being able to make wise decisions and see things clearly, you went through your life in survival mode, not realizing that this way of living has been affecting your life. I wanted to write this because for so many years, I wondered why I made some of the decisions that I made, and what I discovered was that the reason was so much deeper. I want you to take some time and think about all the decisions you've made in your life, and how they affected you. Then I want you to work on getting to the core of the problem. It may take some time, and it may take a couple of counseling sessions; however, instead of telling yourself, "This is my last time. I'm not going to make another bad decision like this ever again," tell yourself, "I'm going to get help because until I get help, I now know that my decisions will constantly get in the way of my happiness because I have not addressed the root cause of my decisions."

When people go through a break-up, they do one or two things: they spend most of their time trying to distract themselves by buying things they don't need and spending money they don't have because they want to prove to their ex-partner that they are better off. They put themselves in debt just to seem happy but internally, they neglect themselves and eventually, they fall into a dark place. See, the one thing about life is that we try to find one million reasons to run away from the real problems. We put on so many masks and we hide behind so much hurt, and because of this, we continuously dig ourselves into a never-ending hole due to the decisions that we've made that have been motivated by bad experiences.

We take a moment to slow down, think and focus. Sometimes we run around so much trying to avoid the problem, staying super busy, maybe even working extra jobs, instead of facing the problem. I've learned that if you don't get to the core of the problem you'll never get better, you will be an example of a person who repeats the same thing and expects a different outcome. I'm not saying that just because you have had some bad experiences, they can be an excuse to do what you want to do. However, what I'm saying is that it's time to work on yourself, it's time for a reality check, and it's time for a wakeup call. Stop blaming your failures on your job, your career, or being underpaid. The bottom line is that you've been spending a lot of unnecessary time and money trying to cover up all of your problems, thinking that you can just make them go away. Many people believe that success cures all our problems, but if you have read my first book, *Give It One More Try*, you know it's not true at all. You need to fix yourself from within, and when you do so, that's when things change and get better.

Here is a list of 26 things that you may not have thought of that may play a direct role in you continually making bad decisions:

1. Growing up in a single-family home
2. Growing up in a poverty-stricken family
3. The amount of emotional support you got from your

parents growing up
4. Trauma you have experienced in your youth
5. Verbal abuse
6. Physical abuse
7. Emotional abuse
8. Broken families
9. Crime
10. Drugs
11. Having parents who show no emotions
12. Being rejected by your parents or someone that you admired
13. Relationship break-ups
14. Hurt
15. Anger
16. Low self-esteem
17. Being bullied at a young age
18. Growing up in a household where no one communicated
19. Age
20. Pride
21. People pleaser
22. Fear
23. Worry
24. Lack of education
25. Loss of hope
26. Low self-worth

I wanted to name these 26 things because I'm certain there's something on this list that you or someone you know have experienced and because of these experiences, it plays a significant role in the decisions that people make in their lives. I want you to always remember that everything happens for a reason and there is a reason for everything. With that being said, make a promise to yourself that you will dig deep to find the experiences that continuously affect your decisions and work on them. It's not going to happen overnight, everything takes time, but if you want to achieve true happiness, you must start digging deep and go to the core of your problems to rebuild yourself. All of this happens once you understand why happiness is the way to go.

The 90 Day Plan

During the next 60 days, write everything you are grateful for each day.

1. _____

2. _____

3. _____

4. _____

5. _____

6. _____

7. _____

8. _____

Why Happiness Is The Way To Go

9. _____

10. _____

11. _____

12. _____

13. _____

14. _____

15. _____

16. _____

17. _____

18. _____

19. _____

20. _____

21. _____

The 90 Day Plan

22. _____

23. _____

24. _____

25. _____

26. _____

27. _____

28. _____

29. _____

30. _____

31. _____

32. _____

33. _____

34. _____

35. _____

36. _____

37. _____

38. _____

39. _____

40. _____

41. _____

42. _____

43. _____

44. _____

45. _____

46. _____

47. _____

The 90 Day Plan

48. _____
49. _____
50. _____
51. _____
52. _____
53. _____
54. _____
55. _____
56. _____
57. _____
58. _____
59. _____
60. _____

During the next 30 days, I want you to come up with a few things that you can start to do to show your level of gratefulness with the blessings that you currently have.

1. _____

2. _____

3. _____

4. _____

5. _____

6. _____

7. _____

8. _____

9. _____

10. _____

11. _____

The 90 Day Plan

12. _____
13. _____
14. _____
15. _____
16. _____
17. _____
18. _____
19. _____
20. _____
21. _____
22. _____
23. _____
24. _____

Why Happiness Is The Way To Go

25. _____

26. _____

27. _____

28. _____

29. _____

30. _____

Afterword

After reading this book, I hope that I have managed to enlighten you on happiness and why happiness is the way to go. In life, for most of us, happiness is what we all want. However, life sometimes takes you in many different directions and within those directions, there's a different experience. The problem with that is we never know what's around the corner, we never know what lies ahead of us—whether good or bad, difficult or challenging—but at the end of the day, happiness is what life is all about. So, when we get pushed in different directions or have let downs in life, it can be the most painful thing for anyone to deal with because it disrupts our happiness, stresses us out mentally and emotionally, and for so many of us, those moments and experiences caused us to be unhappy or lose our happiness. We must remember that outside of any experience, one of the most powerful forces on the earth is the human mind. The mind can send you into places that you wouldn't want to deal with. The mind can also offer you so much joy, peace, gratefulness, and happiness; however, we must be very careful of what we take in, what we allow to enter our minds, and we must be very careful about our thoughts and understand that thoughts impact us in many ways. We must be very careful of the information that we spend the most time taking in.

Throughout my studies on the effects of human thoughts for over 10 years and reading tons of self-help books and books on the mind, I have concluded that life is all about what you make of it. We all have freedom of choice and we all have free will, and at the end of the day, it's up to us to determine if we want to be happy. Our happiness is never dependent upon anyone else. At some point in your life, you realize that happiness is a choice and yes, we all have encountered things that were out of our control, and I understand that. However, there's always help if you're willing to do the work on yourself. There are always resources, there's always a solution, and more importantly, there's always prayer. Your past hurts, mistakes, and failures do not determine your future or your future blessings.

I thank you for taking the time to walk this journey with me on why happiness is the way to go. I hope that happiness, contentment, and gratefulness has moved up to one of the top priorities in your life. I hope that this book has empowered you and opened your eyes. More importantly, I hope this

Afterword

book has convinced you why happiness is the way to go.

Remember, if no one else loves you, God is always love. Trust me, knowing this kept me alive during the tough times.

Notes

Chapter 3: Set Yourself Free

"Positive Psychology Center." *Positive Psychology Center*, ppc.sas.upenn.edu/.

Medical News Today, MediLexicon International, www.medicalnewstoday.com/.

www.ingramcontent.com/pod-product-compliance
Lightning Source LLC
Chambersburg PA
CBHW071236090426
42736CB00014B/3106